Prayers for Young People

# DAVID GATWARD

# Life's Little Questions

Kevin
Mayhew

First published in 1996 by
KEVIN MAYHEW LTD
Rattlesden
Bury St Edmunds
Suffolk IP30 0SZ

ISBN  0 86209 830 0
Catalogue No  1500066

0 1 2 3 4 5 6 7 8 9


Cover illustration by Roy Mitchell

Design by Veronica Ward
Artwork by Graham Johnstone

Edited by Peter Dainty
Typesetting by Louise Hill
Printed and bound in Great Britain

# CONTENTS

# CONFUSED

You got a minute, Lord?
It's about being, well, er, kind of confused.
Everything and nothing is happening
    at the same time!
Decisions to be made.
Work to be done.
Problems to be solved.
Do you understand, Lord?
It's not so much a case of being lost,
    more of a 'spaghetti junction' in life.
Where do I go, Lord?
Where are the signposts?
Which road do I follow?
I've so much I want to do,
    yet so little I can.

Are my thoughts clouded, Lord?
Sometimes I despair.
It just doesn't seem worth it.
I want to run, Lord, get away,
    from you, friends, work, life, everything.
Is it worth carrying on, Lord?
I see no light at the end of the tunnel.
Where are you in this swirling darkness?

Are you testing me, Lord?

It's at times like these that I need you most,
Yet . . . I get no answer.

I don't want to be rude, Lord, but . . .
    do you really exist?
It seems that logically you don't exist,
    yet at the same time you do!
You know what I mean, Lord?
Do you really understand?
Are you confused?
I really wonder sometimes, Lord, whether,
    well you know, what if?
Perhaps . . .
Why?
If only!!
CONFUSED!!

Oh, Lord, help me to untangle
    the lines of my thoughts.
To see your purpose for me ahead.
I don't want to be confused any more, Lord.
It's confusing!!

Amen.

# Prayer

Lord, it's about prayer.
Well, it's just I don't know how to . . .
   well, you know, pray.
What is it, Lord?
How do you start?
What do you pray about?
Who do you pray to?
   God?
   Jesus?
   Father?
   Mother?
   Lord?
   Dad?!!
It's not easy, you know.
There's never been any real guide to follow –
'101 Ways to Pray!!'
Not a bad idea really is it?
It's all very well this Christian stuff,
   but how do you go about it?
Can't you give us even a tiny hint?
You say we should listen.
How do we do that when our minds
   are so full up we just forget to pray? –
   never mind listen!

How do we know if you've heard us?
How do we know if we've been answered?
Do you understand, Lord?
It isn't just me is it?
I often wonder if I'm the only Christian
    doing everything the wrong way!!
But is there a wrong way, Lord?
Is there *any* way?

Bear with me, Lord.
It's tough, but please keep helping me.
Even though I find it all so hard
    I know I'd be lost without you.
You know what I really mean,
    even if my prayers don't say it.
You know what I need,
    not what I think I need.
Help me to trust your decision, Lord,
    even though it might hurt.
Pick me up when I fall down.
Heal my broken faith when I begin to doubt.
Teach me to pray, Lord.
Please!!

Amen.

# PARENTS!

Hi, Lord, got a minute?
Well, it's about parents.
What are they, Lord?
One minute you hate 'em,
    next you love 'em!
'I've been there too,' they say.
Have they?
Are you sure they're not made in
    a 'parent factory'? –
    a production line, each given
    the necessary items for parenthood.
Yet, if that's so, why do they seem so
    incompetent when it comes to us,
    the *adolescents*?
Are we that hard to understand, Lord?
Surely parents are there to help.
Then why do they always seem
    to hinder,
    never understand,
    jump to conclusions,
    and treat you like a child?
I thought they'd 'been there'!

Do you know what I mean, Lord?

They shout and scream at you, saying:
   'I wonder if it's worth it,' or,
   'I wouldn't have got away with that
   when I was your age!'

Teach them to listen, Lord.
To understand.
We know we're not perfect,
   but a little love and
   encouragement go a long way.
We know they love us, Lord,
   we really do.
Without them we'd never pull through.
Just let them know, Lord, how we feel.
And that although we find life difficult,
   we still love them,
   and always will.

Amen.

# GROWING UP

Lord, I'm alone,
  alone in my room.
Shut off from the turmoil
  of the outside world.
The only sound the soft, calculated
  ticking of my clock.
It gives me time, Lord,
  to gather my thoughts:
  the problems of teenage life;
  adolescence.
It's strange, Lord, being 17.
Not an adult and not a child.
Yet expected to be one or the other
  several times a day.
Have adults forgotten that they were
  teenagers once?
Surely they should be filled with advice
  and help?
Yet all they do is shout
  and tell you to 'grow up'.
What is 'growing up', Lord?
If it means becoming like them, Lord,
  I don't want to.
They've stopped growing, Lord.

They think they've arrived.
No more to learn.
I don't want to be like that, Lord.
I want to be 'growing up'
   not a 'grown up'.
I never want to stop learning.
I want to remember what it's like
   being a teenager,
   and be able to understand
   how they feel.
I don't want to forget,
   like so many of the grown-ups today.

Why don't they understand, Lord?
Do we frighten them?
Are they scared of us?
We only want to be heard, Lord,
   understood . . .
   loved . . .

Don't they realise that, Lord?
Are they blind?
I don't think it's us that need help, Lord –
   it's them.

Amen.

# AM I A CHRISTIAN?

Lord, can we talk?
It's about my faith, my belief.
You see, as a Christian
    I'm supposed to 'spread the Word',
    'tell the Good News',
    'bring people to Christ'.

To be honest, Lord, I don't,
    (well at least, not very well).
I'm nervous, scared, embarrassed.
'What will people think?'
'I can't tell them, they'll laugh at me.'

It's quite a problem because for some reason
    people ask, 'Are you a Christian?'
'YES!' I proclaim out loud!
But then they ask, 'Why?'
And that finishes me, I'm done for, trapped,
    a stuttering mass of confusion, lost for words,
    and unable to answer.
    Huh! Some Christian!

I do know why I believe.
(Honest! )

It's just explaining it that's the problem.
Can you give me some help, Lord?
How about a job description, guidelines for
    nervous Christians, things to do, and not to
    do, when confronted by that 'why?'

I really wish I could hold my ground,
    answer their every question,
        speak your truth, proclaim your Word.
Aren't I good enough?
Am I a bad design?
A faulty product?
What am I doing wrong?

Lord, (are you still there?),
    could you give me a hand, please?
I do find it hard to speak out.
So help me when someone asks,
    'Are you a Christian?'
Because maybe if they're asking, their reason
    for doing so might be me, my life,
        and the way I live it with you.
So who knows, Lord,
    maybe I'm getting there after all!


Amen.

## DIRTY FEET

One of the great things about God is that he loves us as we are. We can be the most grotty, disgusting individuals, but God still manages to see us as we might become with his help. He sees the potential me, whilst loving the *actual* me!

There can't be many more irritating feelings than seeing someone tramp dirt through a house that you've just cleaned. In they march, and what was outside on the pavement now firmly sits on your best Axminster! Wonderful! So what do you do? You learn from the experience, you clean up and then make sure that no one else crosses the doorstep without first taking off their shoes. Compare that with God. Imagine him having a house. The front door is open in welcome. Someone strides in with muck all over their feet. They leave their dirt behind them wherever they go. God smiles and invites them into his front room! Of course, the dirty feet are a problem, so he asks the new friend how they came to be so dirty. As the story is told so he listens, and gently begins to clean those feet and wipe the dirt off the carpet.

When the friend steps outside again their feet are clean, unblemished. As they leave so someone else enters, only their face and their hands are as grimy as their feet. And God does the same for them only on a grander scale! Again and again this happens. Old and young, healthy and diseased, they all enter. Some have returned many times, their faces have become well known, the ever-dirty feet only too familiar. God doesn't complain. He just helps us clean up and sends us on our way with renewed confidence and determination to stay that way. He loves us – dirty feet and all!

Lord. Hi!
    About five minutes ago
    something strange happened.
My brother walked into my bedroom.
Strange? No, not usually.
That is, it wouldn't have been
    if he hadn't been carrying an engine
    from a 125 cc motorbike in his arms!
    It brought a smile to my face
    to say the least!
There he was,
    muck and grime all over his shirt.

In his arms – an engine.
And on his face?
The proudest grin I've ever seen.
There it shone for all the world to see.
As if saying, 'Look, Dave! I did it!
    I got it off! Great, eh?'
And it was at that moment it hit me.
What it is to be in a family, all together.
I was writing, but he wanted to show me
    what he'd achieved.


Mum and dad were painting
    the bathroom (how romantic!).
But they also had to share the moment.
You see, Lord,
    we take an interest in each other.
If one does something they're chuffed about,
    then they tell the rest; share the happiness;
    even if it does mean carting a greasy engine
    upstairs into a freshly painted room!!


There are so many homes where you have to
    take your shoes off before you go in.
It's to avoid getting the carpet dirty.
    'Yes, you can come in
    as long as you don't make a mess.'

OK, I'll agree, they're lovely houses.
But they don't feel like homes.
They can be cold,
   clinically clean.

Our house?
Well, we charge in, shoes on, coats soaked,
   and we just plonk down in front of the fire!
Of course we clean our shoes,
   but that's not the point.
The point is that we can come in as we are.
We don't have to discard our rubbish
   at the door
It comes in with us.

A bit like your family, Lord.
You accept us as we are.
Disgusting and grotty.
No sign commanding us
   to clean our feet before entering.

Thank you for that, Lord.
For accepting me,
   dirty feet and all.

Amen.

## Me . . . Myself . . . I

Lord? It's me again.
I'm sitting at my computer,
 in the middle of an essay,
 and I've got a problem.
It could wait.
After all, this essay is for tomorrow.
But I need to talk about this now.
It's bothering me and I need to chat about it.

It's me, Lord, me;
 my self-obsession,
 my self-centredness,
 my infatuation with what is happening to
 me whilst I forget about others:
 my friends, people,
 other people with problems too;
 problems that don't matter
 when compared to mine;
 problems that are quite frankly
 irrelevant when put next to the enormity
 of my own;
 problems which I don't have time
 to deal with at the moment
 because I have 'other things to do';

problems that *they* should be able to
deal with, not dump them on me;

problems that they should put aside
for mine, offer me a helping hand,
give me the pity *they* deserve,
the warmth *they* need to feel,
the hand *they* want to hold,
the shoulder *I* have not offered,
the ear *I* have not opened,
the heart with which *I* haven't even cared.

Because, Lord,
all that is really important
is me,
myself,
I;
my own self-importance,
my own need to be adored,
admired, loved.

I want them to come to me,
to ask *me* how *I* feel,
to know when *I* need help,
when *I* am feeling under the weather,
tired, worn down.

But in this, Lord,
I fail to recognise what they have offered.
In their need I see
   selfishness.
In their loneliness I see
   begging.

So, Lord, I come to you,
   the friend who always listens,
   always helps,
   always waits unquestioning,
   full of love.

And I ask you, Lord,
   that in my selfishness,
   my ignorance of others,
   my self-obsession,
   you will offer me,
   not the helping hand that I myself
   find so hard to stretch out,
   but help me to notice
   the others who are hurting,
   needing me,
   myself . . . I.

Amen.

## DOUBT

Lord,
    it is quiet now
    and I am alone,
    away from the noise,
    away from the people,
    away from the distraction,
    the confusion.

So I am here
    in the darkness of my mind,
    the quietness of my room,
    to talk to you; to listen to you;
    to try and understand.

It seems, Lord, to me,
    that all I ever do is doubt:
    whether it is you or myself,
    my ability or your love,
    your existence or my trust.
I always doubt.

Some say that it is normal,
    that it allows you to question,
    search for a deeper meaning.

But with me it is consuming.
It takes over and I get swallowed.

And as it takes over,
   so my mind loses sight;
   as the paths turn into lost walkways
   and the distant truth flickers and dies.

So why do I doubt, Lord?
Why do I doubt?
Is it because I want everything now
   and get upset when it takes
   that little bit longer?
Is it because I am too easily distracted?
No, Lord.
It is deeper than that.

It is because as I sit here
   and stare into the future,
I see the shadows of my past;
   all the memories of a childhood
   which is fading,
   sinking into the sands of my life.
It is because I teeter on the edge
   of an unknown quantity –
   my life.

It is because I see no escape
   from all the pressures,
   all the problems
   which scream inside my head.
I see no direction,
   no plan, no future.

Yet I know that this is where I must go.

My life leads on into a land
   that as yet I cannot see:
   a land full of ups and downs,
   lies and truths,
   doubts and beliefs.
And it is here that I must go.

So I find that even in my doubt,
   I rely on you:

   the one I lose sight of,
   the one I ignore,
   the one I lose belief in,

   the one that I trust.

Amen.

# IT'S NOT ABOUT BEING PERFECT

Lord,
I'm tired.
I'm tired of the world;
   tired of the pressures,
   the falseness,
   the lack of faith.
I'm sick of it all.

I try.
I really try to follow you,
   to live the way that you taught,
   do the right thing.
And all I do is fail,
   trip up, fall flat on my face.

. . . Do you know what keeps
   tripping me up, Lord?

Not you, not life,
   but the way other 'Christians'
   perceive I should behave, act,
   be 'Christian'.
And I can't.
I can't live up to their expectations.

I'm me;
    full of anxieties,
    problems, lies,
    hidden secrets.

But I still hold on.

I can't pretend to be anything else.
I'm not perfect.
Why should I be?
You never asked me to be.
It's something out of reach.
    . . . and I'm too far away to try.

And I'm sorry, Lord.

But others don't accept that.
They condemn, scorn, judge.

And I crouch in the corner,
    protecting myself:
    what I am,
    from what they want me to be.

I can't be what they want me to be:
totally perfect, clean,

no problems;
    totally, utterly, completely Christian.

And I'm not –
    according to them.

But why?
Because I disagree?
Because I'm not perfect?
Because I break the rules?

But I admit that.
So what's the problem?
Didn't you come for sinners?
    for the lowest of the low?

I'm fed up, Lord,
    fed up with all these hidden judgements.
'If you are a Christian you should be perfect.'
But Lord, I'm only young.
I've my whole life ahead of me.
If I stopped making mistakes now,
    struggling, arguing,
        what would I have left to learn?

If I stopped questioning,

going my own way,
how would I be able to experience
life to its full?
If I stopped being
what you created me to be,
what would I have left to give?

I live.
I experience.
Life is not about being perfect,
it's about learning,
following, following . . .

Lord,
I am not perfect.
I break the rules,
walk my own way,
ignore you, shut you out.
But I admit that.

I admit that I am nothing special.
I can't live up to what is expected;
be perfect;
stop doing all those 'unchristian' things.
I'm human –
a human in a world of confusion.

Yet I still hold on to your hand.

When I'm lost,
   when I'm cold,
   when I find myself alone,
   kneeling, crying,
I know you'll be there.

I know that you love me.
That no matter what I do
   no matter how sad or pathetic I become,
   that you'll be there, and you'll pick me up.

So, Lord,
   in my world,
   a world being destroyed
   by ideals that I follow –
   even though I may be wrong,
   I know that you want me to keep going.

So, Lord, I pray,
   'Don't give up on me.'

Amen.

## DISAPPEARING UNDIES!

Lord,
I did my washing today!
HURRAH!
But somehow,
    (and I really don't understand this),
    my underpants are missing.
And so are three socks.

Do you know where they are?
You see, Lord, it's one of those
    bizarre occurrences.
You know you put them there.
You are sure that they were spotted
    entering the washing machine,
    being shoved into the dryer,
    yet,
    against all the laws of nature,
    you open up the bag when you get home
    and lo and behold . . . they are gone!

They that were there
    are no longer in your possession.
They have taken it upon themselves
    to explore further avenues of work,

explore the world,
go out and meet other single pieces
of underwear!

Weird.

Where on earth did they go?
Is this another one of those hilariously
    amusing heavenly humours?
Another angelic jape?
Something to tickle the ribs
    of all wearers of halos?

(Imagine losing *those* in the wash!)

I know you have a sense of humour,
    a definite interest in the sublime
    and divinely daft.
One only need look at other
    classics of God-funniness –

    acne,
    men having nipples,
    my face.

You are one comical creator!

So where do they go, Lord?
Why do they disappear?
Are they all in heaven?

And that's why I'm praying, Lord;
Not because I want my underpants back,
    (although it would be helpful),

but just to say thanks for giving us all
    something to laugh at – from people to places,
    jokes to japes, laughs to tears of happiness,
    and back to my disappearing undies!

If at the end of my life
    I can look back with you, Lord,
    sitting down around an old camp fire,
    crack open a bottle of wine,
    and,
    amongst all the mistakes,
    the mess,
    the problems,
    the pain,
    see the fun as well,
    I will know that I have lived . . .

Amen!